ANCIENT GREECE

FARMERS & FIGHTERS

Jane Shuter

Heinemann Library
Des Plaines, Illinois

03 02 01 00 99
10 9 8 7 6 5 4 3 2 1

Library of Congress Cataloging-in-Publication Data

Shuter, Jane.
    Farmers and Fighters / Jane Shuter.
       p.   cm. -- (Ancient Greece)
    Includes bibliographical references and index.
    Summary: Examines the two main occupations for men in ancient Greece where only Sparta had a full-time army while soldiers from all other city states were also farmers.
     ISBN 1-57572-737-4
    1. Greece--History--To 146 B.C.--Juvenile literature. 2. Greece--History, Military--Juvenile literature. 3. Agriculture--Greece--Juvenile literature. [1. Greece--History--To 146 B.C. 2. Greece--History, Military. 3. Agriculture--Greece.] I. Title.
II. Series: Ancient Greece (Des Plaines, Ill.)
DF89.S54 1998
355'.00938--dc21

                         98-7149
                         CIP
                         AC

Acknowledgements
The Publishers would like to thank the following for permission to reproduce photographs:
Ancient Art and Architecture Collection pp. 5, 21; Antiken-sammlungen, Munich p. 16; Art Institute of Chicago p.25; Ashmolean Museum p.8; Bildarchiv Preussischer Kulturbesitz p. 15; British Museum pp.20, 23, 29; C.M. Dixon pp. 9; Wadsworth Atheneum p. 7.

Cover photograph reproduced with permission of Bildarchiv Preussischer Kulturbesitz.

Every effort has been made to contact copyright holders of any material reproduced in this book. Any omissions will be rectified in subsequent printings if notice is given to the Publisher.

Any words appearing in the text in bold, **like this**, are explained in the Glossary.

CONTENTS

MOUNTAINS AND SEA

Greece is a country broken up by mountains and the sea. In ancient times, it was hard to get from one place to another. It was a long time before the Greeks thought of themselves as part of one country, even though they spoke the same language and had the same religion.

Timeline

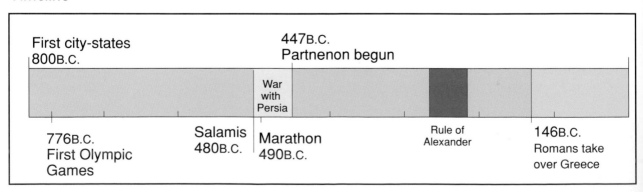

First city-states
800B.C.

447B.C.
Partnenon begun

War with Persia

776B.C.
First Olympic Games

Salamis
480B.C.

Marathon
490B.C.

Rule of Alexander

146B.C.
Romans take over Greece

CITY-STATES

If people did not see themselves as Greek, what were they? Most people were part of a **city-state**, which was a city and the land surrounding it, and most of them were farmers. City-states were small and some only had a few thousand families. Athens and Sparta were the biggest and most important city-states.

Different city-states were run in different ways. Some had one **ruler** who was usually a king. Some were run by the most important men. Some were run by most of the free men of the city, the men who were not **slaves**. All city-states expected the men to fight when there was a war. This book looks at two main occupations for men in Ancient Greece, fighting and farming.

The mountains of Greece were dry as well as steep. This meant that it was very hard to grow crops there.

Most men in a **city-state** were expected to fight when there was a war. Women, the sick, or the disabled, did not fight. The soldiers had to bring their own weapons. **Archaeologists** have found remains on Greek battlefields. The remains show that some soldiers were in their teens and others were over fifty years old.

PART-TIME FIGHTERS?

Sparta was the only city-state with a full-time army. Other armies had soldiers who were also farmers. They could not fight all year round. They had to be at home during busy times of the farming year, such as harvest time. Spartan soldiers had sayings like, "Come back with your shield or on it." This meant they should either win (losers threw their shields away and ran) or die (the dead were carried home using their shields as stretchers). Part-time soldiers had a different view of the matter as this poem shows:

A perfect shield is worn by some Thracian now.
I had no choice; I left it in a wood.
Oh well, I saved my skin, so let it go!
A new one's just as good.

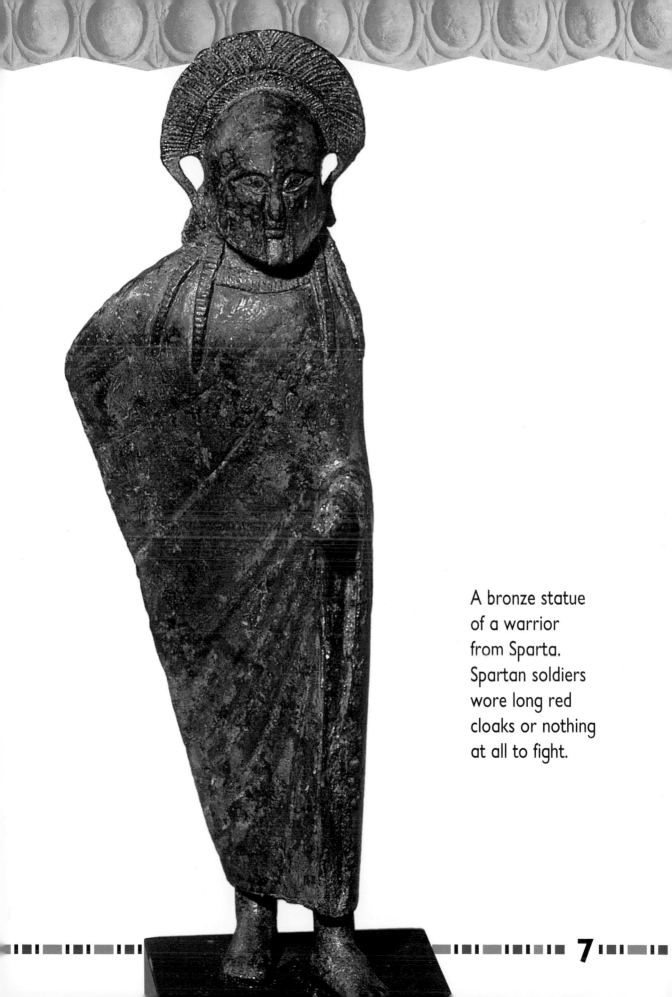

A bronze statue of a warrior from Sparta. Spartan soldiers wore long red cloaks or nothing at all to fight.

War was part of Greek life. Most Greek men expected to go to war regularly in their lifetime, just as they expected to marry and have children. **City-states** often fought each other. Sometimes they **traded** with each other and joined together to fight another city-state. Small city-states that were close to Athens or Sparta usually agreed to join them. They would probably have been forced to fight anyway. A small city-state would see an advantage in joining a larger one because the larger one would protect it.

If another country invaded Greece, many city-states might fight together. But when the enemy was beaten, they soon began to fight each other again.

A toy war chariot. Most Greek boys played with toy weapons and soldiers. Children's fighting games made it easier for them to train for real war later.

These archers are part of the wall decoration from a Persian temple showing all kinds of Persian soldiers. The Persian army fought and dressed very differently from the Greeks.

THE PERSIANS

Persia was Greece's nearest and most powerful neighbor. The Persians were a constant threat, even when they were not invading. They invaded Greece in 490 B.C. (under King Darius) and in 480 B.C. (under Darius' son, Xerxes). The Greeks beat them back both times.

Greek land battles were fought mainly by **hoplites**, who fought standing shoulder to shoulder so their shields made a wall against the enemy attack. There were about six rows of soldiers. Those at the back pushed the rest forward. If a soldier fell, another one stepped from behind into the gap. If the wall of shields broke, the soldiers were easily killed and the battle was lost.

MARATHON, 490 B.C.

In 490 B.C., a huge Persian army landed at Marathon, about 25 miles (40 kilometers) from Athens. It had about 20,000 **archers**, men with spears, and horsemen. Athens and the small **city-state** of Plataea had only 10,000 men. Sparta promised to help but had to finish several days of **religious ceremonies** first. By the time they arrived, it was all over. First, both armies just watched each other for several days. Then the Athenians made a surprise attack. The battle was long and hard, but the Athenians won. About 6,400 Persians and 192 Greeks were killed. The dead were buried under a mound that is still there today. For years, the Athenians were angry with the Spartans for not coming to help at once.

The battle of Marathon

At first, the Greeks fought at sea by getting close enough to the enemy ships for their soldiers to fight. But they found that sea battles could be won more easily by **ramming** enemy ships. The Greeks soon had several kinds of ships in sea battles. There were small, fast ships to take messages and big, heavy ships to ram. The heavy ships (triremes) had as many as 170 men rowing them. With many oarsmen, the ships went faster and rammed harder.

SALAMIS, 480 B.C.

In 480 B.C., the Persians invaded and took over parts of Greece. They beat the Spartans at Thermopylae. They marched on to Athens. About 400 Persian ships also sailed to Salamis off the coast of Athens. About 300 Greek ships were waiting. They trapped the Persian attackers in a narrow channel and sailed up to make a line across it. A Greek playwright described a Persian view of the battle:

The Greek ships were in a circle around us. They closed in and rammed. Our ships turned over; the sea was choked with wrecks and slaughtered men. The beaches and low rocks were covered in corpses.

The battle of Salamis

Because Greek people fought so often, their doctors had a lot of practice treating wounds. Even in the earliest battles, there were doctors on the battlefield. There was often one soldier in every group who was good at caring for wounds. They tried to clean the wounds, often with wine, which stops **infections**. They also gave the wounded soldiers herbs in wine to make them sleepy and soothe the pain. They used the same herbs in ointments for the same reasons.

BATTLEFIELD MEDICINE

IN ABOUT 760 B.C., A GREEK WRITER NAMED HOMER WROTE LONG STORIES ABOUT ADVENTURES AND BATTLES. HE ALSO MENTIONS BATTLEFIELD DOCTORS:

Agamemnon commanded the doctor be brought to Menelaos, who was wounded by an **archer**. The arrow was still in his wound. When he came to where Menelaos was wounded, he took out the arrow. But the pointed sides broke off in the wound as he did so. He skillfully sucked them out and then put on a soothing ointment that he carried with him.

This decoration from the bottom of a Greek drinking cup shows a soldier bandaging a friend's wounded arm. The arrow he has pulled out of the wound is near the injured man's knee.

EVIDENCE FROM THE TIME

We know about the **armor** Ancient Greeks wore and the weapons they used because some of them have survived. There are also vase paintings that show soldiers. Writings from the time also tell us about the armor they wore and how they fought.

IN ABOUT 760 B.C., A GREEK WRITER NAMED HOMER WROTE LONG STORIES ABOUT ADVENTURES AND BATTLES:

At last the armies met with a clash of shields, spears, and bronze-covered fighting men. The **bosses** of their shields collided and a great roar went up.

A vase painting of a hoplite. He is putting on his armor.

NEW EVIDENCE

Each time **archaeologists** excavate a battlefield, they find armor from the time that they can study.

A Spartan buried on a recently excavated battlefield had an iron spear point still in his chest. This shows that if a spear was pushed hard enough, it could go through the bronze chest armor that **hoplites** wore.

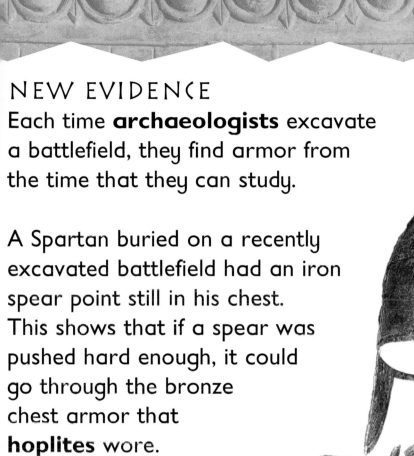

Some hoplite helmet and chest armor. When it was being used, it would have been polished until it was shiny.

In the past and today, the land in Greece is hard to farm. A lot of it is too dry and hilly to grow more than olive trees and **vines**. Ancient Greek paintings show farmers growing **crops** with very simple wooden tools.

THE FARMING YEAR

The farmers plowed the fields and sowed the seeds in October, just before the rain that would help the seeds grow. The **grain** was harvested in May. In September, they harvested olives and grapes, which they made into oil and wine. They also grew other fruit, beans, and vegetables that were ready in September.

IN ABOUT 700 B.C., A GREEK WRITER NAMED HESIOD DESCRIBED THE LIFE OF A FARMER:

There will be no rest ever from toil and hardship during the day nor from suffering at night. You must work to avoid **famine** and earn the love of the corn goddess who will fill your barns. After the harvest, there may be time to rest in the shade of a rock with wine and goat cheese.

Farmland surrounded
the cities in city-states.

Farmers grew **grain**, fruit, and vegetables on the flat land around the cities. Greece did not have much land that was good for growing **crops**, so **city-states** often found it hard to grow enough food for everyone. This was especially true of the big city-states such as Athens. City-states often had to **trade** the **goods** they made a lot of (like oil and wine) for food from other countries such as Egypt.

These men are harvesting olives by hitting the branches with sticks. Ripe olives fall to the ground to be collected. Greek farmers still harvest olives in this way.

MOVING ON

Between 700 and 500 B.C., many groups of Greeks moved to live and farm in other places. There was not enough land in Greece for all of them to farm. The first of these **colonies** was in Italy. The Greeks set up colonies along the Mediterranean coast and around the Black Sea. People in these colonies kept their Greek ways. They traded some of the food they grew with Greece (usually with the city-state they had left).

A pottery model of some women making bread, a very important food. Most city-states had to buy grain from other countries so that everyone would have bread all year round.

KEEPING ANIMALS

Cattle were used to pull **plows**. Goats were kept mostly for milk and cheese, and sheep were kept for wool that was spun into thread. Animal skins were made into leather for shoes and clothes. Chickens were kept for eggs and were eaten when they stopped laying eggs. Bees in hives made honey to sweeten food and drink.

MEAT

The Greeks did not eat a lot of meat. They sometimes ate chicken or goat. They ate meat mostly after **religious ceremonies**, when animals were **sacrificed** then eaten afterwards.

THE GREEK WRITER HOMER DESCRIBES A SACRIFICE BEFORE A BATTLE:

When they had prayed and scattered grain, they slit the throat of an ox for sacrifice. They skinned it and burned the thighs and entrails as a sacrifice. They cut the rest into small pieces, put them on sticks stripped of leaves, and roasted them over a fire. Then they ate the meat and shared it equally between them.

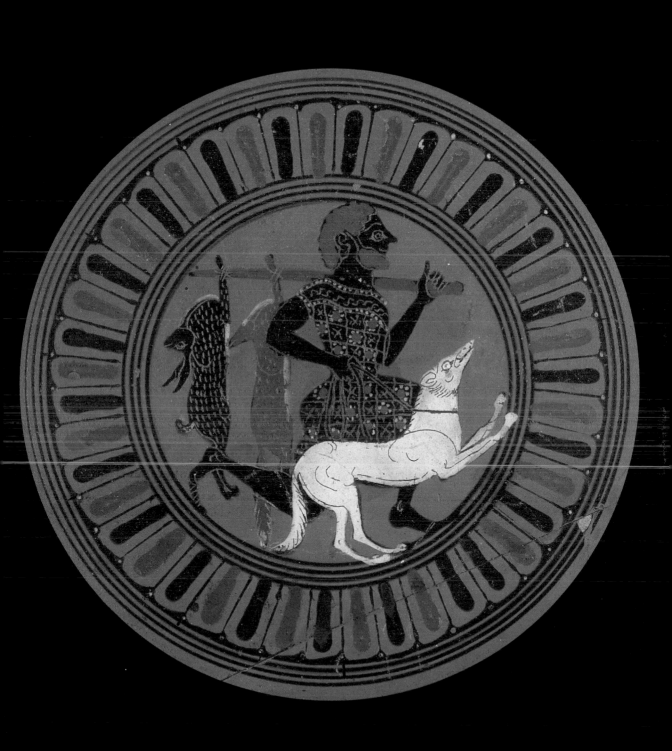

The Greeks often hunted wild
animals for fun and for meat.

FOOD: FISH

ALL KINDS OF FISH

In Ancient Greek times, seas and rivers of Greece were full of fish. The Greeks ate a lot of fish. Fish was not often given as a **sacrifice** like red meat. Instead, it was eaten as part of ordinary meals almost every day. The Greeks ate fish, squid, octopus, and shellfish. They roasted them, grilled them, and baked them with sauces. They ate them hot or cold.

CATCHING FISH

Ancient Greek paintings show fishermen catching fish in nets from boats and lobsters in cages made from twigs. People also fished with a fishing line and a pole.

TRICKING CUSTOMERS

People in the cities bought fish from the market. The fish was brought in early in the morning from fishing villages along the coast. Plays from the time talk about fish sellers in markets pouring water over their fish to make it seem fresher than it really was!

ONE OF THE EARLIEST RECIPES EVER WRITTEN DOWN IS FROM GREECE IN ABOUT 400 B.C. IT IS A RECIPE FOR COOKING FISH:

Cut off the head of the ribbon fish. Wash it carefully and cut it into slices. Pour cheese and oil over it. Bake it.

Ancient Greeks ate fish from this plate. It is decorated with a painting of the perfect catch!

STORING

Wine, water, and oil were stored in large pottery jars. Many of these jars have survived. Fish was dried or preserved in oil in jars or bottles. **Grain** was bought and **ground** into flour for bread nearly every day. It was stored in bins in barns on farms.

COOKING

The Greeks cooked food over an open fire or in the oven. Ovens were mostly used for bread. Most cooking, roasting, grilling, and boiling or baking in pots was done on metal grills over an open fire. This could be done inside or outside depending on the weather. Ordinary people probably had a cooking **hearth** outside and in a corner of their main room. Bigger houses had a kitchen.

Food is prepared in an Athenian town house

ORDINARY MEALS

Breakfast was usually just bread and cheese or fruit. This was the midday meal too, perhaps with some fish or vegetables left over from dinner the day before. The main meal of the day was eaten in the evening. People ate fish, vegetables, and bread. Ordinary people did not eat meat except at **religious ceremonies**, unless they caught a wild animal. Richer people might eat some meat, such as sausages, chicken, or small wild birds. They only ate lamb, pork, beef, or goat at **feasts** or religious ceremonies.

DINNER PARTIES

Men often had dinner parties, which women and children could not attend. The servants cleared away food while the guests sat and drank wine. They ate and drank lying on couches. Women entertainers danced and played music for them.

A male dinner party. The men took off their shoes and lay on couches while they were entertained by musicians and dancers.

archaeologists people who dig up and study things left behind from past times

archer a soldier who fights with a bow and arrows

armor coverings for different parts of the body to protect soldiers in battles. Armor is usually made of metal.

bosses protective metal piece in the center of a shield

cattle cows and bulls

city-state a city and the land it controls around it

colonies places set up in one country by people from another country

crops plants that farmers grow for food or to use in other ways (to make clothes, baskets, or paper)

famine a time when there is not enough food and people die of hunger

feast a special meal with a lot of different things to eat and drink. Feasts often celebrate special days.

goods things that are made, bought, and sold

grain types of grasses with fat seeds that are eaten. Barley, wheat, rye, oats, and rice are all grains.

ground crushing grain up until the seeds are a powder (flour)

hearth a flat bed of stones for lighting a fire on

hoplites soldiers who fought on foot with spears

infection germs that get into wounds and makes the patient sick

plow a tool that turns over the soil to break it up

ramming sailing straight at another ship and running into it to try to sink it

religious ceremonies special times when people go to one place to pray to a god or goddess

ruler the person who runs the country

sacrifices something given to a god or goddess as a gift. If the sacrifice was a living thing, it was killed before it was given.

slaves people who are treated by their owners as property. They can be bought and sold and are not free to leave.

trade there are two meanings: a job; for example, "Shoemaking is his trade" or, selling or swapping goods; for example, "Greece traded oil for grain."

vines the plants that grapes grow on

wounds injuries

INDEX

MORE BOOKS TO READ

Dawson, Imogen. *Food & Feasts in Ancient Greece.* Parsippany, NJ: Silver Burdett Press. 1995.

Nardo, Don. *Ancient Greece.* San Diego, CA: Lucent Books. 1994.

Steele, Philip. *Thermopylae.* Parsippany, NJ: Silver Burdett Press. 1993.

Zinovieff, Sofka. *Greece.* Danbury, CT: Franklin Watts Inc. 1997.